Bead Soup:

Devotions for Jewelry Artists
(or anyone who loves jewelry)

Marci Perrine

DEDICATION

I would like to dedicate this book to my Lord & Savior Jesus Christ who died to save me.

CONTENTS

Acknowledgments i

1 My Testimony 1

2 All About The Pearls 6

3 A Price Far Above Rubies 10

4 Pure Gold 14

5 Accessorize 19

BONUS Jewelry Tutorial 24

About the Author 32

ACKNOWLEDGMENTS

I want to thank my wonderful husband Phillip for encouraging me to write this book. I want to thank my awesome kids who daily provide me with inspiration. Finally I want to thank my Pastor who preaches the Word of God and lives as a great example of a true Christian.

Chapter 1

My Testimony

Before you begin working with wire, make sure you have all the proper tools. Chain or flat nose pliers, round nose pliers, and wire cutters are all essential.

In your Christian life it is just as important to have proper tools. You need your Bible and prayer time along with a good Bible believing church in which to attend.

My Testimony

As I sat at my desk crying, I couldn't stop thinking about the words I'd heard the evangelist speak the night before. "Are you a sinner?" All I knew was that God was convicting me, and I needed to respond. Sure, I grew up in a Christian home. I'd been faithfully serving in the church for as long as I could remember. I'd made at least two professions of faith as a child, and I was pretty sure I was saved. I had even been baptized. It would be shameful if everyone thought I had been lying all these years. Well, I didn't lie on purpose, but it had been a lie none-the-less. I was not saved. God was pricking my heart and I knew it. It would be much worse to continue living a lie than to just accept Christ as my savior. I needed to swallow my pride.

As I cried through the rest of the day, I knew I needed to be saved. Instead of turning my car toward home that evening, I drove to my pastor's house. I started to feel some peace. I went inside and spent time in Bible reading and prayer with his wife, and that very evening I asked Christ to come into my heart and save me. Guess what!... He did!

I was 21 years old and I felt like I had just been born. Why? I felt this way because I was born again. It was an awesome feeling and I want that for every one who reads this story.

How do you get saved and receive Christ as your savior? It's as easy as ABC!

A – Admit you are a sinner. Romans 3:23 says, "For all have sinned, and come short of the glory of God." That means that it doesn't matter who you are. You may be rich or poor, black or white, a decent person or a drug addict. The Bible says "all" have sinned. We are all equal where this is concerned. Not only do you need to recognize that you are a sinner, but you really need to have true repentance. You need to tell God how very sorry you are that you have sinned against Him.

B – Believe on the Lord Jesus Christ. Romans 10:10 says, "For with the heart man believeth unto righteousness…" You see, since we are sinners, God cannot just let us into heaven. Sin cannot enter in the kingdom of God. However, God says that He is not willing that any should perish, but that all (there is that word again) should come to repentance. He also says in Romans 6:23, "For the wages of sin is death; BUT the gift of God is eternal life through Jesus Christ our Lord." How can God let us into heaven? He sent His son to take our place of punishment. Jesus died on the cross and shed His blood to cover our sin. "For without the shedding of blood, there is no remission…"

C – Confess unto salvation. Romans 10:10 continues on to say, "…and with the mouth confession is made unto salvation." We should not be ashamed of Christ. We should boldly proclaim His name.

Put it all together. Romans 10:9, "That if thou shalt confess with thy mouth the Lord Jesus, and shalt believe in thine heart that God hath raised him from the dead, thou shalt be saved." There is no magic in a prayer. All of this comes from your heart. However, I want to lead you in a sample prayer if you have never asked Jesus to come into your heart to save you.

Dear Lord Jesus,
I know that I am sinner, but I no longer want sin to control my life. I am very sorry for all the sin that I have committed and I turn to you now. I believe that you died in my place on cross. Please come into my heart now and save me. In Jesus name I pray, Amen.

If you truly prayed this prayer and believe that Jesus has saved you, I urge you to let someone know. I also urge you to find an Independent Fundamental Baptist Church as soon as possible so that you can become grounded in the Word of God.

ABC's of Jewelry Making
Always Be Creative!

Acrylic
Beads (of course!)
Charms
Dichroic
Eye pins
Findings
Glass
Head pins
Inlays
Jewelry
Karat
Leather
Mandrel
Needle
Oxidation
Precious Gems
Quench
Round- nose Pliers
Stones
Tutorials
Unique Items

EWELRY

Vivid Colors
Wire
Xilion
Your Style
Zoo of Choices

Learning Like Children... I am a home schooling mom, and I really love it! And, what does that have to do with making jewelry? Everything!!! First of all, I got started in jewelry making a couple years ago when a fellow home schooling parent taught a class on basic beading. Many of the parents bring their kids together on Fridays for 3 months in the fall and 3 months in the winter/spring. Then several different parents teach classes for other kids and adults depending on their skill set. I taught American Sign Language since my first passion is working in the Deaf community and I am fluent in this language. Anyway, back to the learning. I am so glad that I participated in this jewelry class as it gave me the confidence to go out and start learning more on my own.

After taking this class, I started to get interested in wirework. I saw some incredible wirework as I surfed the internet. To my amazement, I fell in love with this craft. Well, how did that happen? I did something that I see my children do all the time. I get a little bit of interest in something, and then I research everything I can on that subject. When my kids are interested in something, they want me to help them look up information on the internet, or go get books on the subject. They will try to get examples of whatever it is, and play around with it. This is just so fun!

My daughter loves to paint, and at only 7 years old, has all her own grown up painting supplies. She wants every painting kit she sees from the kid's kind to the adult kind. So, if it's within the budget, we get it for her. I don't make her stay within the confines of the picture, either. She takes art classes at the same place we go on Fridays. She looks for paintings that she can study and learn from. She amazes me. Well, I did the same thing with wire. I went out and purchased several different gauges and kinds of wire. I didn't get the expensive precious metals or anything. They are too rich for me yet. I got some flat nose pliers, round nose pliers, and wire cutters. I bent, curled, swirled, read free tutorials, played some more, cut, played, read, etc.

Now, in those first days, I didn't really make anything exciting. What I did was learn! I learned how the wire felt in my hands. I learned how it would look if I bent it certain ways. I learned how it looped and bent with my different pliers. Finally, I learned that it wasn't nearly as scary as it looked.

I still have that same passion for working with wire as I did when I began. I'm constantly seeing what I can make that's new and unusual. I love buying new tutorials and learning new techniques, but nothing can beat those first few days when I was just absorbed in learning how the wire moved. If you are new to any craft including wirework, beading, polymer clay, metal smithing, rock polishing, or whatever, then the best thing to do before you get good and started is just to play. Get to know the product you are working with and have fun!!! I promise, it will make you a better artist in the long run.

As Christians, we can learn this way as well. Just dive into God's Word and ask Him to guide you. Go to church and listen to great preaching. Meet with other Christians and share fellowship. All of these things will help you grow as a Christian!

Chapter 2

All About the Pearls

 There are two types of pearls. One is formed in salt water while the other is cultivated in fresh water. Salt water pearls are generally perfectly round balls while fresh water pearls come in all different shapes and sizes.

Most jewelry artists cannot afford to work with real salt water pearls but will instead use glass faux pearls or fresh water pearls.

 The next few devotions will be written around the theme of pearls. Follow along closely to see what can be gleaned and how they will help us in our walk with the Lord.

Forming the Pearl

A pearl is formed when a foreign object ends up inside an oyster or a clam shell. This object may be no smaller than a grain of sand. It becomes an irritant inside the shell. At that point, the crustacean starts to coat the foreign object with something called nacre. As the shell fish continues to coat this irritant, something starts to happen. This foreign object that started out as an irritant or a problem starts to become a beautiful shiny object. The nacre has formed a pearlescent coating that becomes a precious jewel that can be made into a piece of art.

 Did you know? – Perfectly round pearls are very rare, and therefore the term "pearl" has become a metaphor for something special or unique.

Isaiah 53:5 says, "He was wounded for our transgressions, he was bruised by our iniquities..." Just as the oyster never did anything wrong, Jesus Christ was perfect in all ways. Yet he was brutally punished for sin. His sin? NO! He was punished for our sins. When I think of this oyster, he lived a life in pain to bring forth a very rare and expensive gift. In fact, he had to give his life in order to give that gift. This is what Christ did. Through his death he gave us the gift of eternal life. Now, just like any gift, we have to receive it in order for it to belong to us.

 Dear Heavenly Father,
I want to thank you for the rare and precious gift that you have given through your son Jesus Christ. Not only have our sins been forgiven, but we have been given eternal life and you have made us meet to be partakers of the inheritance of the saints in light. You have delivered us from powers of darkness and we are so appreciative. (Col 1:12-13) Thank you Father. In Jesus name we pray. Amen!

Imitation Pearls

"Although imitation pearls look the part, they do not have the same weight or smoothness as real pearls, and their luster will also dim greatly." (http://en.wikipedia.org/wiki/Pearls) Keep this definition in mind as I tell the following story. (Original author unknown)

One day a little girl was shopping with her mother. She saw a pretty pearl necklace that was made just for little girls. She wanted it really bad and so she asked her mother if they could buy it. Not one to spoil her daughter, the mother agreed to get it, but only if the girl would earn it. She had to do some chores around the house and save up her allowance.

After a couple of weeks, the little girl had earned enough to pay her mother for the pearls, and she was so very excited. She wore those pearls everywhere. She slept in the pearls, and played outside in the pearls. The pearls had dimmed over time, but oh, she still loved her pearl necklace that she had worked so hard for.

One night, as was usual, her daddy came in and read her a story. However, before he left the room, he asked the little girl if she loved him. She said that of course she loved him. He asked her to give him her pearls. She cried and said, "Oh no, Daddy, not my pearls! I love my pearls. Please don't make me give them to you." The daddy told her that was okay, and she didn't have to give him the pearls.

Her daddy waited another week before he asked her again, but, as before, she cried begging him to ask for anything else, but not her pearls. This continued for several weeks.

After one such night, after he had tucked the little girl into bed, he was surprised to see her peek her head around the corner with tears running down her cheeks. He called her over to comfort her and to find out what was wrong. The little girl held out her hands and said, "I'm sorry I wasn't willing to give you my pearls, Daddy. I do love you and know you wouldn't ask for them unless there was a good reason." As the little girl handed over her pearls, her father pulled out a rectangular box and handed it to his beautiful daughter. When she opened the box, she pulled out a strand of bright beautiful pearls. They were the real thing!

Daddy said, "I was waiting for you to grow up enough to give up the childish set of pearls so that I could give you the real thing."

I have always loved this story. The daddy never forces the child to give him the pearls, but waits for her to realize how much he loves her and would never do anything to cause her pain. He wants her to give up the imitation because he wants to give her the real thing.

Wow! How many of us do the same thing? We hold onto the cheap imitation things of this world when the Father loves us so much that He wants to give us the real things of life. The things that are eternal. Do we love Him enough to trust Him? Paul writes in I Corinthians 13:11, "When I was a child, I spake as a child, I understood as a child, I thought as a child: but when I became a man, I put away **childish** things." As we mature in the Lord, he expects us to put away those childish things. So ask yourself this question. Do you have imitation pearls, or are you ready for the real thing?

Dear Heavenly Father,
I know there are things in this world that I am often not ready or willing to give up. But I pray that you would touch my heart about each of these things that I would instead desire the real things that you have prepared for me. Help me to serve you with my whole heart.
In Jesus name I pray, Amen!

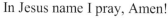

Of all the gemstones, pearls are the least durable. Although they can get dirty just like any other piece of jewelry, care must be taken when cleaning and preserving them.

Put your pearls on very last after preparing for the day. After putting them on, don't apply makeup, put on perfume or body or hand lotion. At the end of the day, wipe the pearls off with a dry cloth. If pearls become dirty, don't used harsh jewelry cleaners or otherwise. Only use very mild soap with a damp cloth to gently clean your beautiful pearls.

~We have tender and sensitive hearts that also sometimes need cleaning. I am so thankful that God in all His wisdom will gently pick me up and clean me up as necessary!~

Chapter 3

A Price Far Above Rubies

 **How the price of a Ruby is determined**. Rubies are priced on a number of different characteristics. Taken into consideration are the cut, clarity, color, and carat. On this particular website, I saw tiny flawed rubies all the way to large rubies that were nearly perfect in every way. The ranges in price were from $167 all the way to $3,249. Wow! (gemsoul.com)

The Virtuous Woman

"Who can find a virtuous woman? For her price is far above rubies." We should all strive to be this Proverbs 31 example of a wife and mother. As I read through the list of this virtuous woman, I found there were times that I matched the things that she did, but so much more often, I fall short. When God talks about a virtuous woman having a value far above rubies, he is telling us that we can't put a price on the things that a wife and mother do. I have heard of women, when forced into divorce court, being accused of just "staying at home." I have heard about some of these women getting clever and giving a bill to the husband since he found her staying at home to be of little worth. The prices on these itemized bills were up into the $100,000,000's. Why? Well, if you are a wife or mother or both, then you know why. Here is what Proverbs says about the virtuous woman.

1. She is trustworthy
2. She will always be good to her husband
3. She has a job whether at home or outside the home

4. She gets up before dawn to start her day
5. She prepares good meals for all those in her household
6. She takes care of the finances
7. She takes care of herself that she can stay healthy
8. She has a side business of selling things to help with the income of her home
9. She sews for her family
10. She helps with the poor and volunteers her time
11. She is not worried about cold weather as her family has everything they need
12. She dresses nicely
13. Her husband is well known and respected because she only talks kindly about him
14. She has strength and honor in character
15. She always talks kindly and speaks only wisdom
16. She always makes sure that the house is well maintained and is not idle
17. Her children rise up and call her blessed and her husband also
18. Many daughters have done virtuously, but you excel them all
19. She is well known and liked in the community
20. **She fears the Lord above all**

I don't know about you, but this list is very hard to live up to. Look at number 20 on the list. This is the most important thing that is said about this virtuous woman. Without the Lord's help, you can accomplish nothing. I think this was put near the bottom because that is what sums up the entire list above it. I fail every day on many of these things. We can never perfectly fulfill them all. In fact, we won't be perfect until we reach heaven. Sin reigns in these old bodies, but one day we will have a glorified body. Until then, I can strive to be the Proverbs 31 woman with God's help.

Dear Heavenly Father,
In Proverbs 31 you have provided us with an outline on how to be Godly wives and mothers. Though we are not perfect, we pray today that you would help us to do your will in every part of our lives. Help us to live so that our children and husband can call us blessed. Most importantly help us to live a life that is pleasing to you. In Jesus name I pray, Amen!

One of the rarest rubies in the world was a pear shape ruby and was 102 carats. This sold for $12,750,000. Rubies are the next hardest gem next to diamonds. Diamonds are a 10 on the MOHS chart while rubies are a 9. Rubies can range in color from almost pink to a deep fiery red.

The Price of Wisdom

When preparing for Bible studies or Sunday School classes, one of my favorite things to do is word studies. Looking up the definition of a word can really give you some insight to what God wants you to understand. The word of God tells us to "study to shew thyself approved unto God." (II Tim 2:15) Without a clear understanding of the scriptures, there is no way to gain real wisdom. Wikipedia defines wisdom as "a deep understanding and realization of people, things, events or situations, resulting in the ability to apply perceptions, judgments and actions in keeping with this understanding." How can we have Godly wisdom without using the word of God in these perceptions, judgments, and actions? It is highly important to spend time in prayer and study. Job 28:18 states that the "price of wisdom is above rubies." By now we have established that rubies are very expensive. So, it is costly for us to gain wisdom. It costs us our time more than anything. Pro. 3:13-15 tells us that "happy is the man that findeth wisdom..." because "it is more precious than rubies." Since a virtuous woman and wisdom are both more expensive than rubies, I would say that these two ideas go hand in hand. We need to use wisdom in all areas of our life, but without Godly wisdom there is no wisdom at all.

Dear Heavenly Father,
I pray that as I study your word I would gain Godly wisdom. Help me as I learn and grow to have spiritual perception, discernment, and judgment. As I gain wisdom, let me not become proud, but always to stay humble as Godly wisdom only comes from you. In Jesus name I pray, Amen!

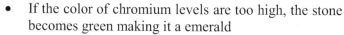

More Ruby Facts

- Ruby is a result of the mineral corundum
- The red color is because of the presence of chromium
- If the color of chromium levels are too high, the stone becomes green making it a emerald
- Another variety of this same stone is sapphire
- The only other precious stone besides these three is the diamond
- Rubies range in color from bright pink to dark fiery red
- Ruby is the birthstone for the month of July

The Ghosts of Jewelry Past I am being haunted. "What is haunting me?" you ask. Of course it is my jewelry foibles and flops!

I was looking through some old jewelry that had at one time been put out for sale. Back when I made these pieces, I thought they were awesome. Now, almost 2 years later, I'm not so sure. So, what can I do with these "interesting" experiments? Hmmm.... I have a few ideas. I could call ghost busters, but I doubt that would help. Maybe I could have an exorcism and salvage the souls (or in this case the beads) of the pieces. Maybe they just need an extra blessing and re-working. Should I just ignore them and maybe they will go away? That seems unlikely.

Then there are the pieces that you start and you just can't seem to finish. I have a whole box full of these. They call to me daily. "Please, finish me." These are the pieces that just don't seem to be going as well as they looked on paper or in the tutorial. I really don't know what to do with these. So, they remain in the unfinished box (or in the coffin). Maybe someday I will have enough experience to go back and raise them from the dead. Until then I will just mourn what could have been.

Chapter 4

Pure Gold

 Gold mined out of the ground and in the river does not come out in a pure form. It is often attached to other ores such as silver, iron, and copper. It has to go through a purification process that is actually a little more complicated than I once thought. Later in this chapter I will go into more detail about that.

I Shall Come Forth As Gold

Job 23:10 says, "But he knoweth the way that I take: **when** he hath tried me, I shall come forth as gold." Have you heard the saying, "tried by fire"? Well, I believe this is what Job is talking about here. He had just lost everything he had including all his children, all his servants, all his money, and finally his health. His wife just wanted him to curse God and die, but Job was so faithful to God that he knew that wasn't the right thing to do. Job was a righteous man. Not a perfect man, but a righteous man. He knew that God had a purpose in the trials that he was put through. God has only our good in His plan as is stated in Romans 8:28. "For we know that all things work together for good to them that love God, to them who are the called according to his purpose." When Job talked about being made as gold, he meant that God was purifying him. What do we have in our lives that may need to be purified? We can work on getting it out now as the Holy Spirit gently speaks to our hearts or we can wait until God allows us to go through the fire.

Dear Heavenly Father,
I pray that you will touch my heart with the impurities that I need to get out of my life. I pray that as you need to allow me to go through the fire that I will realize it is only for my good and for your glory. Help me to shine and reflect your light as only pure gold can do. In Jesus name I pray, Amen!

Gold Made Pure

When gold is purified it is put into a large vat where it is heated to the melting point. Once the gold is melted, then a salt solution is added to the gold. This is the exciting part… The impurities from the gold cling to the salt solution. It is actually the salt that pulls the impurities out of the gold. Now, let's compare our hearts to the gold. As our heart goes  through the fire, it is made ready to add the salt solution or the Word of God. Without the salt, the impurities would just stay in the gold. That's just like our hearts. With the salt of the Word of God the impurities are removed. When the gold has been in the fire long enough, the salt solution is scraped off taking with it all but maybe about .5% of the impurities. Our life on earth will never be completely perfect, but we need to let the Word of God constantly work to purify our hearts.

 Once again we come to you Father asking that you work in our hearts. We know that through the trials and tribulations in our life you are working to purify us. We know that without your Word, this process cannot happen. Only when we submit to your will can we come forth as gold for you. Thank you Father that you love us enough to do this. In Jesus name I pray, Amen!

Percentage of Gold by Karat

When a piece of gold refers to the number of karats, it's actually telling you how much gold is in the piece. 24 karats is almost 100% pure gold. However, it is extremely soft and delicate. So, many times gold is mixed with other metals to make it more durable. Below is a table showing the amount of gold present in specific karats.

24k	99%
21k	87.5%
18k	75%
14k	58.5%
10k	41.7%

10K gold is the lowest grade gold that can be sold in the United States and still called gold jewelry. Anything less than this will probably just be gold plated.

Walking On Streets Of Gold

The Word of God tells us that the heavenly city is made of gold so pure that it is like transparent or clear glass, and yet we will be walking on this pure gold as the streets are also paved with it. (Rev. 21:18-21) Even though the Bible describes heaven, I just can't quite imagine what it will be like. God's glory will be brighter than sunlight and will light that city. There are twelve gates to the city and each one is made of a solid pearl. The walls and the foundations are made of all kinds of precious gems. In heaven, these are the building blocks instead of wood, bricks, and cement. Here are on earth we put so much emphasis on our riches and all these precious things, and yet in heaven there will be an endless supply. Our God is so wonderful and generous. The things that we know about heaven should make us want to serve Him here on earth. Are you building up earthly treasure or are you building up heavenly treasure? Col 3:2 tells us to "set our affections on things above, not on things on the earth." If your goal is heavenly treasure, then you need to be about the Father's business. Are you telling others about Him? Are you spending time with Him in prayer and Bible study? If not, then your affections are right here around you.

Precious Heavenly Father,
What a sight we will have to behold as we enter the gates made of pearl. In the mean time, I pray that you will help me spend more time with you and have my affection set on heavenly things. Help me to not be so concerned about setting up my treasure here on earth. In Jesus name I pray, Amen!

New Year's Resolutions... Jewelry making quickly became my obsession! Then when I discovered wire, I became a lost cause. My husband, who used to be an electrical technician, was really impressed with my knowledge of gauges, tools, etc. Once I discovered a wonderful jewelry making website, I knew I had found an awesome community of obsessive jewelry makers like myself.

Well, we all know the famous resolutions made around New Year's. After all the holiday parties and festivities you may be vowing to lose weight, drink more water, or exercise more. However, how many of you make New Year's resolutions when it comes to jewelry making and business? Last year I decided that I would take a year off from tutorial making in exchange for learning new techniques and becoming stronger in the things that I already knew. I think that in the last year I have done exactly that. I believe that I have come a long way this year in the execution of my projects.

About mid-year, my favorite jewelry site came out with the premium membership. I signed up on day one! When I saw all that was being offered, I knew this was going to be something that would be very beneficial. I have not been disappointed. I can't wait to see what 2013 has in store for this great site. I am now taking a jewelry design course and I feel like I am learning so much from this, and I encourage anyone not already utilizing this tool to start now.

So, what new goals do I have for this year? First of all, my resolution for this year is to write at least one new tutorial per month. Next, I want to learn at least one new technique per month. I don't care how advanced you think you are, you can always learn something new. Third, I promise to write at least one article per month. I've really taken a shine to writing! Fourth, I am going to start blogging on Facebook on my jewelry page. Fifth, I will keep my Facebook store and my internet store more up to date each month.

How can the above article be applied to your Christian life? We should constantly be evaluating ourselves using the Word of God. We should vow to study to become better Christians. We should set goals that relate to memorization of scriptures, time spent in prayer, etc. Only you and God can determine what you need to work on. These are the true resolutions that matter. My resolutions that are about jewelry making are great, but the ones that I make to become a better Christian are far more important. ***Write down at least 3 things that you can do to improve your walk with God.***

Chapter 5
Accessorize

Many of us like to accessorize by adding jewelry to our wardrobe. My favorite accessory is rings, but I wear all types of jewelry. I wanted to find out what the Bible says about jewelry or accessories. This being the final chapter of this book, I thought it would be fun to show you, the reader, the interesting things that I found out.

A Servant Forever

In Old Testament times, it was not uncommon for people to made slaves or servants of their own race of people. I was reading in Deut. 15:16-17 and found something really great. After six years of serving a master, the master can let him go free. However, if he really loves the master, he can choose to stay with him forever. In this case, the master will use an aul to pierce the servants ear. This marks the servant as belonging to the master. Are you about to shout with excitement yet? Do you see where I am going? I love my Master, my heavenly Father. I want to be marked as belonging to Him. He loves me and takes care of me. Why would I want to go any other place and serve another master?

Dear Lord and Heavenly Master,
Lord I fully give my heart into your service. Mark me as your own so that others will know who it is I serve. I love you more than any other. In Jesus name I pray, Amen!

I sit down in my thinking chair,
See my tools... I'll use that pair...
Shall I bend the wire in loops and squiggles, or hammer and pound?
Neither one - I'll coil and wrap - less sound!!
Wires and beads, gems and things,
Shall I make bracelets, or some rings?
Buttons, crystals, spacers, stones,
Mama's creating, turn off the phones!
Copper, silver, or bronze will I use...
To leave it plain or patina...so hard to choose.
and what about my favorite beads?
those big, chunky stones, or those tiny little seeds?
All this choice, my minds a mess
I should just start twiddling, then I'll de-stress

This was a poem that was written by me and several of my friends at JewelryLessons.com. I started it in Oct. 2011. I told them that if I ever wrote a book, it would definitely be included. I thought it was a lot of fun.

Our Outward Appearance

After spending time in this book talking about jewelry, you might be surprised at this devotion. While studying for this last chapter, I had to spend more than normal time in prayer and study to be sure I was presenting the scripture in the correct manner. I even sought counsel on the matter, and then I knew exactly where God was leading me. First, I want to assure the reader that God is not against a woman looking her best. He is not against jewelry or fixing your hair nicely. However, God is much more concerned about our heart than anything else. I Sam. 16:7b tells us that, "*the LORD seeth* not as man seeth; for man looketh on the outward appearance, but the LORD looketh on the heart." This helped me to put the following verses into perspective.

II Tim 2:9-10 reveals something very important about a Godly woman.

She should dress modestly, not be overly concerned with having the newest and best hair style and not be flashy with her jewelry and other accessories. A Godly woman represents her heavenly father. Her main goal should be on her inside and not on her outside. As stated above, God is only concerned that your outside reflect your inside.

After reading I Pet. 3:3-4, I really understood the scripture in II Tim. "[3] Whose adorning let it not be that outward *adorning* of plaiting the hair, and of wearing of gold, or of putting on of apparel;[4] But *let it be* the hidden man of the heart, in that which is not corruptible, *even the ornament* of a meek and quiet spirit, which is in the sight of God of great price.

Peter tells us that our ornament should be that of a meek and quiet spirit. Now I wear jewelry and enjoy nice clothes sometimes. I even like to fix my hair up. However, if I spend more time worrying about my outward appearance than I spend worrying about my inward heart, then there is a problem.

 Dear Most Gracious Heavenly Father,

I pray that as I prepare for the days ahead that you would help me to be less concerned about the outward appearance and more concerned about the inward person. Even though I may enjoy pieces of jewelry here or there, let it not be the thing that consumes my time and my life. However, I pray that through all that I do I will become closer to you Lord. In Jesus name I pray, Amen!

All scripture quoted throughout this book has been from the 1611 King James Version of the Bible. My hope is that you will find the Lord through these written pages and that you would grow closer to Him. I have also had a fun time sharing devotions that have been related to jewelry making. I praise the Lord for leading me down this path. I hope to get to work soon on a new project. Please be on the lookout!

Have you ever noticed... ?

Have you ever noticed that artists, crafters, and jewelry makers in particular have some different ways about them? We have some strange notions at times. Look at this list of things and see if you do any of these crazy things. Maybe it will bring a smile to your face, or make think you need to see someone about it. *smile*

Have you ever noticed... that you get a creative thought in the middle of the night, and you know that if you don't go write it down or make it that you will never go back to sleep?

Have you ever noticed... that no matter how nicely you try to grow your nails, they never quite get there because you are constantly denting or tearing them with your wire?

Have you ever noticed... that it's pointless to file that little indentation in your thumb nail because you are just going to be wire wrapping again in a little while.

Have you ever noticed... that you speak this new language of wire gauges and types, findings, and tools, and the rest of the world thinks you've gone insane?

Have you ever noticed... that you need a specific element for what you are creating, and drive an hour away to the all night craft store so you can get started first thing in the morning?

Have you ever noticed... that you run to the craft store or hardware store needing one small item and you leave having spent $150? (And sometimes come away without the item you went there to get in the first place?)

Have you ever noticed... that you need just a small space to keep your things when you first start out, but before long you are taking over the entire house?

Have you ever noticed... that days may have passed and you wonder how your kids or husband (or wife) got fed and taken care of because you haven't made an appearance out of your studio?

Have you ever noticed… that you go to the hardware store and put a pile of tools, wire, and hardware on the counter, and the clerk looks at you funny when you tell him you are making jewelry?

Well, I've noticed these things and plenty more. I had to write this tonight because I'm definitely the crazy one that wakes up in the middle of the night with a thought and can't do anything else until I get it put down on paper at the very least. As I finish writing this it is now 1am, and my husband is snoring across the room. If he wakes up now, he will ask me what on earth I am doing up?! Then he will smile and just go back to sleep. He knows me too well.

BONUS

Wire Woven Bail Tutorial

Supplies List: 18 or 20 gauge wire – 6 inches
24 gauge wire – dependant on weave chosen
Large bead or pendant with front hole or side
hole

Tool List: Wire cutter
Flat nose pliers
Round nose pliers
Metal File (optional)

Beginning Tips:

- Read entire tutorial before beginning
- Gather all supplies and tools before beginning
- I didn't give an amount on the 24 gauge wire because I leave that open to you. I will show you a specific kind of weave, but you should use whatever weave that you like. I used about 2 – 3 feet of wire for my weave with plenty left for tails.
- In order to keep your weaving neat and tight, use your fingernails or flat nose pliers to push them together.

This tutorial has three parts

1. Making the bail
2. Attaching to a bead with a front hole
3. Attaching to a bead with a side hole

Start with a pendant or bead of your choice. It doesn't matter what the size. You could run a cord through this and it would be fine. However, sometimes you want to add a little something more. I like to add bails without doing a full wire wrap sometimes. Now, let's go through the steps to do it!

Making the bail	
	Step 1 Using the very tip of your round nose pliers, bend your 6 inch wire in half.
	Step 2 Leaving a 4 to 5 inch tail on the 24 gauge wire, wrap it around the upper part of the bent 20 gauge wire 5 times as pictured.
	Step 3 Cross over and around to the other side. Wrap another 5 times.

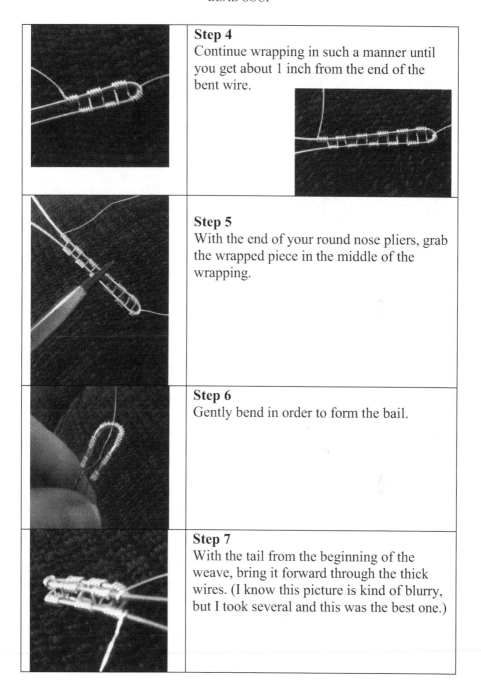

Step 4

Continue wrapping in such a manner until you get about 1 inch from the end of the bent wire.

Step 5

With the end of your round nose pliers, grab the wrapped piece in the middle of the wrapping.

Step 6

Gently bend in order to form the bail.

Step 7

With the tail from the beginning of the weave, bring it forward through the thick wires. (I know this picture is kind of blurry, but I took several and this was the best one.)

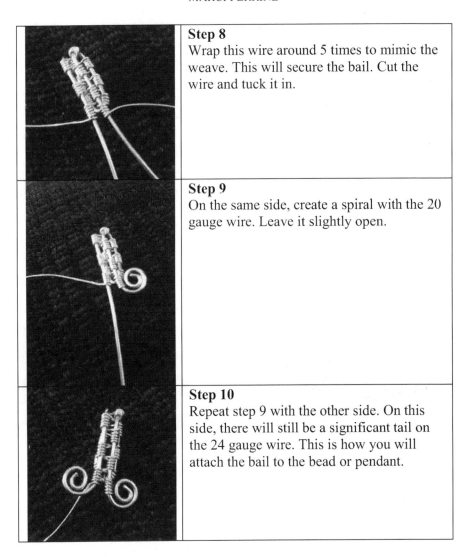

Step 8
Wrap this wire around 5 times to mimic the weave. This will secure the bail. Cut the wire and tuck it in.

Step 9
On the same side, create a spiral with the 20 gauge wire. Leave it slightly open.

Step 10
Repeat step 9 with the other side. On this side, there will still be a significant tail on the 24 gauge wire. This is how you will attach the bail to the bead or pendant.

Bonus:
I will show you step by step how to attach the bail to front drilled beads, and I will show you examples of it attached to side drilled beads.

Attaching to a bead with a front hole	
	Step 11 Slip the loose tail through the front of the bead as shown.
	Step 12 Take the tail wire and put it through the bail as shown. The objective is to wrap it around so that it looks like it's part of the initial wrapping.
	Step 13 After wrapping the wire through the bail, bring it back down and push it back through the hole to the front.

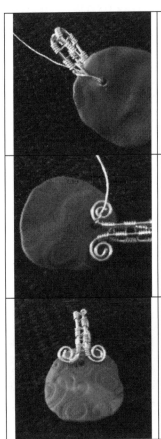

Step 14
After pulling the tail wire through to the front you will begin to wrap it around the inside of the spiral.

Step 15
Wrap the wire around the spiral 5 times. This again looks like a continuation of the weave of the bail. Trim and tuck the wire.

← Your finished bail!

Attaching to a bead with a side hole	
	Step 16 Using the same bail, we will attach it to a bead with a side hole.
	Step 17 Push the tail through the hole.
	Step 18 Proceed to wrap it around the edge of the spiral 5 times or whatever will mimic your particular weave.
	Step 19 Trim the tail wire and tuck in the edge. ← Your finished bail!

ABOUT THE AUTHOR

 Marci Perrine is a Christian serving through Harbor Baptist Temple in Surfside Beach, SC. She is a wife and mother of two beautiful children. Her children are homeschooled, and she enjoys spending this precious time at home with them. Marci works at the church as a song leader/piano player. She is also an interpreter for the Deaf/Hard of Hearing, and has taught children and adult women Sunday School classes. In addition to these many roles, Marci has Life Coach training in which she shares her knowledge and experience in dealing with debilitating illness.

Her newest ventures include jewelry making and design, and writing. Watch for future works from Marci in the form of jewelry tutorials, additional devotional books, Sunday School study material, and finally church plays, programs, and cantata's. Most importantly, Marci wants you to know that she is saved through the precious blood of Jesus Christ, and through her ministry, wants the same for you so that she may see you in Heaven!

https://www.facebook.com/JewelryByMarci

https://www.facebook.com/MyFibroSupport

http://handmadeartists.com/shop/marphilhearts

marphilhearts@yahoo.com

Made in the USA
Coppell, TX
17 December 2024

42853004R00022